*Masonic Symbolism
in
Shakespeare*

By Robert I. Clegg &
William N. McDaniel

Copyright © 2020 Lamp of Trismegistus. All rights reserved. No part of this publication may be reproduced or transmitted in any form or by any means, electronic or mechanical, including photocopying, recording, or by any information storage and retrieval system, without permission in writing from Lamp of Trismegistus. Reviewers may quote brief passages.

ISBN: 978-1-63118-472-7

*Foundations of Freemasonry
Series*

## Other Books in this Series and Related Titles

*The Ceremony of Initiation: Analysis & Commentary*
by W. L. Wilmshurst (978-1-63118-473-4)

*The Old Past Master* by Carl H Claudy (978-1-63118-464-2)

*American Indian Freemasonry* by A. C. Parker (978-1-63118-460-4)

*Some Deeper Aspects of Masonic Symbolism* by Waite (978-1-63118-461-1)

*The Legend of the Holy Grail and its Connection With Templars and Freemasons*
by A. E. Waite (978-1-63118-462-8)

*The Mysteries of Freemasonry & the Druids*
by Albert G. Mackey, Manly P. Hall, &c (978-1-63118-444-4)

*Royal Arch, Capitular and Cryptic Masonry* by various (978-1-63118-425-3)

*The Two Great Pillars of Boaz and Jachin* by A. G. Mackey &c (978-1-63118-433-8)

*Masonic Symbolism of Easter and the Christ in Masonry*
by various authors (978-1-63118-434-5)

*Masonic Symbolism of King Solomon's Temple* by A. Mackey &c (978-1-63118-442-0)

*The Regius Poem or Halliwell Manuscript* by King Solomon (978-1-63118-447-5)

*Psalms of Solomon* by King Solomon (978-1-63118-439-0)

*Freemasonry in the Medieval or Middle Ages* by various (978-1-63118-450-5)

*Masonic Life of George Washington* by Albert G. Mackey (978-1-63118-457-4)

*The Lost Keys of Freemasonry or The Secret of Hiram Abiff*
by Manly P. Hall (978-1-63118-427-7)

*The Kabbalah of Masonry & Related Writings*
by W. W. Westcott, Eliphas Levi &c (978-1-63118-453-6)

*Masonic Symbolism of the Apron & the Altar* by various (978-1-63118-428-4)

*Symbolism and Discourses on the Entered Apprentice, Fellowcraft and Master Mason Blue Lodge Degrees* by various (978-1-63118-413-0)

## Audio Versions are also Available from Apple, Amazon & Audible

# Table of Contents

Introduction...7

*Was William Shakespeare a Freemason?*
by Robert I. Clegg...9

*Shakespeare and Freemasonry*
by William N. McDaniel...25

*The Hiramic Legend*...41

# INTRODUCTION

From the beginning of Modern Freemasonry's birthdate of 1717, the intelligentsia of humanity have found refuge for safe reflection within the walls of the fraternity. Masonic writers have produced a nearly incalculable amount of written musings on a multitude of esoteric and philosophical subjects, as they relate to the ancient mysteries that Freemasonry currently storehouses. Sadly, most of it appears to have sat largely unread, as American Freemasonry in particular, continues to transform itself into something that bears little resemblance to what it was originally designed to be. The true essence of Freemasonry is not that of blind patriotism or a single-minded national religion but one of Universal Brotherhood and altruism, designed for the betterment not just of its members but of society as a whole. In particular, for those who are not members of the fraternity, as Freemasonry has always acted as a beacon, to help guide humanity through darker times, with the hopes that one day we will collectively reach a truly enlightened age.

It's not uncommon for new members joining the fraternity to find little education within the walls of many modern lodges, in spite of so much written material available to the membership. Many older members are not simply uneducated with regards to real Masonic history and symbology, not to mention the vast arena of related subjects, but they are disinterested in all of it, as well.

Lamp of Trismegistus is doing its part to help preserve humanity's Masonic history by making some of these classics available to those students who are seeking to unearth the knowledge of these ancient colossi. As such, Lamp of Trismegistus offers its readers highlights of Masonic study, culled from a variety of authors and viewpoints, with the hope bringing education back into the fraternity. So, be sure to check out other titles in our *Foundations of Freemasonry Series* as well as our *Theosophical Classics, Occult Fiction, Paranormal Research Series, Esoteric Classics, Supernatural Fiction, Studies in Buddhism* and our *Christian Apocrypha Series* as well as numerous other subjects; and, don't be afraid to let a little altruism into your own heart or even into your Lodge. You can also download the audio versions of many of these titles from Apple, Amazon or Audible, for learning on the go.

# Was William Shakespeare a Freemason?

## by Robert I. Clegg

A few pertinent paragraphs from the great Bard, bearing on words and phrases in common use among the Craft:

*"Put on two leather jerkins and aprons."*
-2 Henry IV, II, 2:149

*"They will put on two of your jerkins and aprons."*
-2 Henry IV, II, 4:18

*"Here, Robin, an I die, I give thee my apron."*
-2 Henry VI, II, 3:75

*"The nobility think scorn to go in leather aprons."*
-2 Henry VI, II, 2:14

*"Hold up, you sluts, your aprons mountant."*
-Timothy of Athens, IV, 3:135

*"A carpenter--where is thy leather apron and thy rule?"*
-Julius Caesar I, 1:7

*"Mechanic slaves with greasy aprons, rules and hammers."*
-Antony and Cleopatra, V, 2:210

"*He will line your apron with gold.*"
-Pericles, IV, 6:64

"*You have made good work, you and your apron.*"
-Coriolanus, IV, 6:96

"*Being then appointed Master of this design.*"
-Tempest, I, 2:163

"*The singing Masons, building roofs of gold.*"
-Henry V, I, 2:98

"*Who builds stronger than a Mason?*"
-Hamlet V, I, 47

"*Creaking my shoes on plain Masonry.*"
-All's Well That Ends Well, II, 1:31

"*You shall see him in the triple pillar of the world.*"
-Antony and Cleopatra, I, 1:12

"*And set it down with gold on lasting pillars.*"
-Tempest, V, 1:208

"*And call them pillars that will stand to us.*"
-3 Henry VI, II, 3:87

"*He is not our Craft's Master.*"
-2 Henry IV, III, 2:297

> "*Wooing poor craftsmen.*"
> -Richard II, I, 4:28

The above very interesting compilation appeared in the March, 1918, issue of the Rob Morris Bulletin, the bright publication of Rob Morris Lodge, Denver, Colorado, and is of course the production of its able editor, Henry F. Evans. One cannot but wish that our excellent brother had had the space and time to elaborate his article at such length and skill as his sound Masonic knowledge and literary capacity fully warranted. Then indeed we should have the more nearly arrived at a solution of the really knotty question behind the references he has patiently assembled and which but whet our curiosity to a keener edge. There is no present intention to offer a complete answer to the query. At the best we can but carry forward the inquiry a short stage or two but we shall feel quite content if we attract attention to the problem.

We are also denied the satisfaction of going thoroughly and definitely into explanations. This cannot be done in print. The reader must read between the lines. He must make his own references. If his remembrance of ritual is hazy and incomplete there is but one remedy, get the co-operation of some well-informed Mason, or better still, take the article over to the lodge and read it to the brethren. Their reaction will help. There is wisdom in the counsel of many.

Neither shall we on the present occasion delve into the peculiarities, political or otherwise, of the Elizabethan era. We have pointed out on another opportunity the Craft relation of the gilds and their pageantry and we shall curb our temptation to go deeply into Shakespeare's acquaintance with the trades and their customs. To take but the single instance, William Blades has put on record so many allusions to the one trade, printing, that Shakespeare might from the testimony of his literary output be set down not unfairly as an exponent of that calling.

How much did he know of Freemasonry? We may perhaps meet the inquiry by submitting such evidence as shows what he knew of things and of practices that especially concern Freemasons. Obviously these can be but fragmentary and merely suggestive.

Clarence tells us of King Edward's mysticism in these terms:

*"Hearkens after prophecies and dreams;*
*And from the cross-row plucks the letter G."*
-Richard III, I, 1:54

One might infer that the allusion is to some means of divination, forecasting the future, as the term "cross-row" is to be found explained as meaning the alphabet. Sometimes the alphabet was accompanied with a cross in the old primers or was arranged in the form of a cross as a token of good luck. But the choice of the letter "G" is significant.

Falstaff's death gives in a word by Mistress Quickly, "chrisom child," (*Henry V, II, 3:12*), a striking comparison. Knowing the fullness of the reference the Freemason can with

Shakespeare see the larger vision. For the child when christened was given a white garment and anointed with oil, the while was said the following prayer, "Receive this white, pure and holy vestment, which thou shalt wear before the tribunal of our Lord Jesus Christ, that thou mayest inherit eternal life. Amen." After the member of the Craft has thought over the Apron lectures of Brothers Strobo and Shaver, and also conned over the color allusion by Stowe, "Chronicles of London," to the gifts of the godfathers of "christening shirts with little bands and cuffs, wrought either with silk or blue thread," he will see no doubt what Shakespeare saw, the dying of an old man like unto an innocent child, as one wearing and deserving the purity badge of an Entered Apprentice, "went away an it had been any chrisom child."

Praise to excess is often spoken of as if it were laid on with a trowel. So does Shakespeare speak of it with reference to that very working tool of the Craft, see "As You Like It," I, 2.

Our friend and brother, the great Pythagoras, was by no means unknown to Shakespeare who mentions him by name and alludes familiarly to the theories associated with his school of philosophy. For example:

> "*To hold opinion with Pythagoras*
> *That souls of animals infuse themselves*
> *Into the trunks of men.*"
> - Merchant of Venice, IV, 1:131

Another instance is in "Twelfth Night," IV, 2:49:

*"What is the opinion of Pythagoras concerning wild fowl?"*
*"That the soul of our grandam might haply inhabit a bird."*

Transmigration of souls is elsewhere mentioned by Shakespeare, as in the "Tempest," IV, 1, and in "Hamlet," IV, 5. That beautiful if fanciful -certainly not unscientific- idea, "the music of the spheres," was also Pythagorian and well-known to Shakespeare. Thus it is said in the "Merchant of Venice," V, 1:67:

*"There's not the smallest orb which thou beholdest,*
*But in his motion like an angel sings."*

Does Shakespeare allude to the North? Yes, he deems it the place of darkness and of evil. He mentions a devil assigned to the north. The spirits, "I Henry VI.," V, 3:6, are sought "Under the lordly monarch of the north." See also "I Henry IV," II, 4, and the "Merry Wives of Windsor," II, 2.

There is a noteworthy passage in "King John," IV, 2:197:

*"And when they talk of him they shake their heads*
*And whisper one another in the ear;*
*And he that speaks doth gripe the hearer's wrist,*
*Whilst he that hears makes fearful action,*
*With wrinkled brows, with nods, with rolling eyes."*

The sight of the open hand, as in the outstretched hand when extending it to clasp that of a presumed friendly acquaintance or raising the hand when taking an oath in a court of law or elsewhere or when elevating the hand in giving a military salute or answering one, all these and similar acts had a wider meaning in the days of Shakespeare than is even now known to many of the profane. Then it was not uncommon to brand criminals or otherwise maim or mutilate them. The word "stigma" means such an effect as if burned deeply by fire. Just as the mutilated criminal showed that those in authority had branded him noticeably to the end that the beholders could never mistake him for one unrestrained and unrestricted, free of birth and will, so the person born deformed or accidently so was deemed thus crippled or defaced by the will of God to designate his evil nature. Accordingly in "Richard III," I, 3:228, the hunchbacked Duke is called:

> *"Thou elfish-marked, abortive, rooting hog!*
> *Thou that was sealed in thy nativity,*
> *The slave of nature, and the son of hell."*

Bacon, about the same period, and by the way we will not here venture into a discussion of the true authorship of the plays of Shakespeare, but Bacon refers to the deformity of the body accompanying a perversion of the mind. Thus, agrees Shakespeare:

> *"A fellow by the hand of nature mark'd,*
> *Quoted, and signed, to do a deed of shame."*
> -King John, IV, 2:230

> *"And the blots of nature's hand*
> *Shall not in their issue stand;*
> *Never mole, hare-lip, nor scar,*

> *Nor mark prodigious, such as are*
> *Despised in nativity."*
> -Midsummer Night's Dream, V, 1:399

> *"But thou art neither like thy sire nor dam;*
> *But like a foul misshapen stigmatic*
> *Mark'd by the destinies to be avoided*
> *As venom toads, or lizards' dreadful stings."*
> -3 Henry VI, II, 2:138

Probably an allusion to the branding by a heated crown is indicated by the words in "Richard III," IV, 1:58. Assuredly there is some ground for the belief that some regicides, notably the Earl of Athol executed for the murder of James I. of Scotland, were tortured with a circlet of hot iron around the head. Note the passage:

> *"I would to God that the inclusive verge*
> *Of golden metal, that must round my brow,*
> *Were red-hot steel, to sear me to the brain."*

There is a classic story of the tree that revealed to Aeneas the murder of Polydorus in discovering the grave of the one so patiently sought. The account is to be found in Virgil or Dryden's translation of that author, III, 22. Shakespeare seems quite familiar with it. Thus in "Macbeth," III, 4:122, referring to the fact that murder will out, we are told:

> *"It will have blood; they say, blood will have blood;*
> *Stones have been known to move, and trees to speak;*
> *Augurs and understood relations have*

*By magot-pies and choughs and rocks brought forth
The secret'st man of blood."*

The symbolism of the glove is all but lost among Freemasons, not so in the days of Shakespeare. There was a time when the giving of a pair of gloves to the newly-made Mason was as significant as was the bestowal of anything else. Not infrequently a second pair of gloves was given the new member to be in turn transmitted to the one he loved best of the opposite sex. Today the Freemason is mainly accustomed to the white gloves as an appropriate emblem of mourning to be worn at a Masonic funeral or as adding a touch of Masonic uniform or "clothing" at any other ceremonial of a public character. Shakespeare refers to the gloves as a favor to be exchanged freely by friends but when once acquired and worn it could only be demanded as the act of an enemy. For instance:

*"Give me any gage of thine, and I will wear it in my bonnet; then if ever thou darest acknowledge it, I will make it my quarrel."*
*"Here's my glove; give me another of thine."*
*"There."*
*"This will I also wear in my cap; if ever thou come to me and say, after tomorrow, 'This is my glove,' by this hand, I will take thee a box on the ear."*
-Henry V, IV, 1:261

Appropriately enough from a Masonic point of view where the glove has equal weight with the apron in symbolism, Shakespeare calls it "honor's pawn," and a "token of honor," as may be seen by an examination of "Richard II," I, 1; "Richard II," IV, 1; "Timon of Athens," V, 4.

We are taught as Masons that the form of a lodge is oblong; its length from east to west, in breadth from north to south, as high as heaven, and as deep as from the surface to the center. Thus are we shown the universality of Freemasonry and that a Mason's charity should be equally extensive. But the expressions must sound strange to the young Freemason, much more strange than they would have been to the ears of Shakespeare. He uses east to west in the same limitless fashion thus:

"*O heaven, that such companions thou'ldst unfold,*
*And put in every honest hand a whip*
*To lash the rascals naked through the world*
*Even from the east to the west!*"
-Othello, IV, 2:164

And as to the center, pray consider the following:

"*As true as steel, as plantage to the moon,*
*As sun to day, as turtle to her mate,*
*As iron to adamant, as earth to the center.*"
-Troilus and Cressida, III, 2:172

There is also the claim of the self-confident Polonius who says:

"*I will find*
*Where truth is hid, though it were hid indeed*
*Within the center.*"
-Hamlet, II, 2:156

While dealing to some extent with the points of the compass we must not overlook the location of graves upon which there is an interesting note in Tylor's "Primitive Culture," vol. 2, page 423. He says,

> "*It is not to late and isolated fancy, but to the carrying on of ancient and widespread solar ideas, that we trace the well known legend that the body of Christ was laid with the head toward the west, thus looking eastward, and the Christian usage of digging graves east and west, which prevailed through medieval times, and is not yet forgotten.*"

He also quotes an old work to the effect that the laying of the head to the west was for the purpose that the dead should rise looking toward the east. Did Shakespeare know of this centuries-old belief? He did, as may be seen from the following, relative to the burial of the dead:

*"Nay, Cadwal, we must lay his head to the east;*
*My father has a reason for't."*
-Cymbeline, IV, 2:255

On many occasions we have called attention to the punishment by drowning, the tying of the culprit to a stake at low water and then leaving the body there for at least the period of a couple of tides. Around this old English treatment of criminals grew up certain expressions and superstitions of the liveliest interest to we Freemasons. They are duly noted by Shakespeare. Thus of a rascal in the "Tempest," I, 1:54 it is said:

*"Would thou might'st lie drowning*

*The washing of ten tides!"*

And in the "Midsummer Night's Dream," III, 2:382 we find:

*"Damned spirits all,
That in cross-ways and floods have burial."
Falstaff's death is said to have been:
"Even at the turning o' the tide."*
-Henry V, II, 3:13

And, in the passing of the king in "2 Henry IV," 4:131, is thus recorded by Shakespeare:

*"The river hath thrice flow'd, no ebb between;
And the old folk, times doting chronicles,
Say it did so a little time before
That our great grandsire, Edward sick'd and died."*

Of symbolism we have a wealth of references, too many for easy selection. In mere allusion to numbers there is too large a choice as the mention of significant numerals is extensive. Threes, sevens and nines are noted as of special importance by Shakespeare, as truly they are to all Freemasons. In fact he has put into the mouth of Falstaff, "Merry Wives of Windsor," V, 1:3, an explanation with which we may conclude this compilation:

*"They say there is divinity in odd numbers,
Either in nativity, chance or death."*

Of the symbolism of numbers much is taught in Freemasonry. Three, five, seven, nine, and their multiples are frequently met. All have a pertinent significance for the persevering student of the message shown and conveyed by symbolism. Among the manifold references it is well to reread in this connection the information to be found in the Mackey-Hughan Encyclopedia, Hastings' Dictionary of the Bible *(the article on "Number")*, and Morals and Dogma *(page 548 et seq)*.

Was Shakespeare aware of the peculiar associations that these particular numbers have for many if indeed not all of us? It is very likely that he was so informed. The obvious fact that these numbers are uneven was not unnoticed by him. Nay, he goes further and speaks of odd numbers in a way indicating his acquaintance with the beliefs that had grown around them through the ages of mankind's infancy and mental growth.

So magical was the impression of odd numbers that Shakespeare to the better suggests the uncanny. He puts into the mouth of a witch the two words "one" and "three" where four is meant:

*"Thrice and once the hedge-pig whined."*
-Macbeth, IV, 1:2

In this he had classic authority for his guide. But there is another example of very considerable interest from our point of view. This is in the promise made by Cade to Dick, the butcher of Ashford. Butchers in the reign of Elizabeth were forbidden to sell during Lent unless by dispensation. Cade therefore makes a double promise, to lengthen Lent and also grant a very unusual permission to kill. The number in the promise could have obviously been one thing as another were it not for the deeper meaning associated with the odd number.

> "Therefore, thus will I reward thee
> the Lent shall be as long again as it is; and thou
> shalt have a license to kill for a hundred lacking
> one."
> -2 Henry VI, IV, 3:5

There are instances where the uses of the expression has indeed become so fixed a custom and habit in our conversation that the symbolism and strength of lore is no longer noted by us. Yet even here it is well worth the notice that Shakespeare prefers to employ an odd number where with equal ease he might have used something else. As:

> "Threescore and ten I can remember well:
> Within the volume of which time I have seen
> Hours dreadful and things strange: but this sore night
> Hath trifled former knowings."
> -Macbeth, II, 4:1

Shakespeare has also reproduced an old charm or spell that may have been employed as an agency against attacks of nightmare. Here it is as will be seen the mention of a number is in both cases to an odd one:

> "S. Withold footed thrice the old;
> He met the night-mare, and her nine-fold;
> Bid her alight

*And her troth plight,*
*And, aroint thee, witch, aroint thee!"*
-King Lear, III, 4:120

# Shakespeare and Freemasonry

## by William N. McDaniel

> *We have set it down as a law to ourselves to examine things to the bottom, and not to receive upon credit, or reject upon probability, until these have passed a due examination.* —Bacon's Natural History

Anything proposed at this late day as a new contribution to the history and purpose of Freemasonry should be accompanied by the best of credentials. And yet the very fact of its being new may preclude almost any evidence except what it bears within itself; so that the most one can do is to state what appears to be a truth, show how it has become such to him, and then rely upon it being apprehended by others.

In offering to the Craft this essay, which in its main proposition may seem altogether new, and perhaps revolutionary, all that is asked for it is the application of a primary Masonic rule of action. A strange brother coming into a community is not received as such on his own representation, but neither is he discarded. Let the same method by which he is duly accepted as a member of the Fraternity be applied to the views here expressed. It is the only way in which they will become true to other persons.

Should these views appear to any reader like an attempt to overthrow some of the most ancient landmarks of the Fraternity, the assurance is given that such is not the writer's purpose. Rather it is an effort to restore to the Order the original patent or charter of Freemasonry, thus making it possible to verify or correct all its landmarks.

In reflecting upon the work in Lodge meetings, and its exemplification in the lives of brethren, these questions often presented themselves: What is the purpose of it all? Is its full purpose understood? Are the results commensurate with the ideals of expectations? And to answer these questions was not an easy matter. There is a feeling abroad, which must be widespread, as its expression can be traced through many Masonic journals, that something is wanting in the working of the Order; either there is a misconception as to its origin and object, or errors have crept into the exposition of the work. At any rate it seemed worth some study to ascertain whether there might not be a reasonable explanation for such conditions.

It is apparent to many of the most zealous and loyal Masons that the discussions and uncertainty as to the origin of their Order is placing it on the defensive, and is a handicap to its progress. In these days of libraries and general reading, the influence of standard works of popular education cannot be ignored. At the beginning of the article on "Freemasonry," in the New International Encyclopedia, after a passing reference to the claims made for the antiquity of the Order, the statement is made that "*the Order, however, is now considered to have been instituted about the early part of the eighteenth century - the pretensions put forth to a date coeval with the building of the Temple at Jerusalem, with King Solomon as its first Grand Master, being considered by those who have thoroughly investigated the subject as not worthy of credit.*"

In the new Encyclopedia Britannica the article on "Freemasonry" was written by William James Hughan, recently deceased, a recognized authority on questions pertaining to Masonry. After noting that the Mother Grand Lodge is that of England, which was inaugurated in the metropolis on St. John Baptist's day, 1717, and that a Grand Lodge was founded in Ireland in 1725 and in Scotland in 1736, he states "*it is important to bear in mind that all the regular Lodges throughout the world, likewise all the Grand Lodges, directly or indirectly, have sprung from one or the other of these three governing bodies named.*" Continuing he says: "*It may be a startling declaration, but it is well authenticated, that there is no other Freemasonry, as the term is now understood, than what has been so derived. In other words, the Lodges and Grand Lodges in both hemispheres trace their origin and authority back to England for working what is known as the Three Degrees, controlled by regular Grand Lodges.*" Yet in face of all this the general work and reputation of the Order is based on the assumption that modern Freemasonry is something very ancient.

Studies extending over a number of years led to a generalization so remarkable that at first it seemed incredible, as no doubt it will to many other persons; but it grew so clear and definite, accounting for an origin of the Order consistent with the known facts, furnishing a reasonable explanation for the difficulties which beset it, and giving such an exalted conception of Freemasonry, that its truth could scarcely be questioned.

A point was reached where there was no avoiding the conclusion that the teachings and purpose of Shakespeare and

Freemasonry are identical; that their origin was coincident, or nearly so, the Order being designed to prepare a special body of men to exemplify in actual life the principles embodied in the plays; and, reciprocally, the plays being intended to supply, with concrete illustrations, correct rules of conduct and life; and that both are parts of the grand and comprehensive philosophical scheme of Francis Bacon to regenerate the world and unite mankind into a universal brotherhood.

This view of Freemasonry places it at the very top of that vast scheme, making the institution a necessary integral part of the wonderful plan, without which it would have been incomplete. This view makes the purpose of the Order the most sublime conception of man, being no less than to secure and maintain the freedom, the welfare and the very preservation of the human race. A little reflection will convince any member of the Order that its work has tended toward that end, but what has been done, notable as it has been, is hardly more than a beginning or earnest of what it was meant to accomplish.

To show how such conclusions were reached naturally is:

*"a chronicle of day by day,*
*Not a relation for a breakfast."*

And yet it may be possible to give in a reasonably small compass at least an intelligible, if bare, outline of the course which led up to it.

It is but fair to remark that others have had suspicions or intimations of some close relation between Shakespeare and Freemasonry. The Worshipful Master of Bard-of-Avon Lodge claimed Masonic fraternity with Shakespeare, thinking that allusions to Masonic terms and customs are scattered through the plays, but chiefly on the strength of Hubert's words in King John:

*"They shake their heads,
And whisper one another in the ear,
And he that speaks doth grip the hearer's wrist."*

That action being symbolic of the Sublime degree. Of course this is but a slight and superficial argument, since such actions are not peculiar to Masons.

Frederick Nicolai, a learned book-seller of Berlin, advanced the belief that Lord Bacon, influenced by the writings of Andrea, the alleged founder of the Rosicrucians, and of his English disciple, Robert Fludd, gave to the world his "New Atlantis," a beautiful apologue, in which are to be found many ideas of a Masonic character. But in his opinion the Order was not established until 1646, when a number of men met for that purpose. It is worth noting that this is the same year in which the Royal Society was founded. Had Nicolai understood the relation between Shakespeare and Freemasonry, and the part they bear in Bacon's system of philosophy, no doubt he would have made a different guess.

In the effort to establish the truth of the main

proposition - the identity of Freemasonry and Shakespeare - let all questions relating to their history be laid aside for the present, and let attention be directed to their actual nature. Long ago the wise man who, it is believed, knew all about these subjects, said: "The nature of everything is best considered in the seed"; that is, by beginning with the elements of which it is composed. This course is pursued in all the investigations of modern science, and it should be the proper course for Speculative Masonry. That is the significance of the term Speculative.

It will hardly be questioned that the whole system of Freemasonry is the expansion of some principle, some fundamental idea, just as truly as the mighty oak has developed from the germ within the acorn. Now, the germ idea of Freemasonry is contained in one paragraph of the Charges of a Free-Mason (1723), and in the first line - "A Mason by his tenure is obliged to obey the moral law." And as the embryo of the acorn sends roots down into the ground for the sake of the tree that grows above, so the observance of the moral law is to the end that mankind may be united into one brotherhood - a high ideal, never to be attained, but still the goal toward which to strive. While the main part of this Book of Constitutions pretends to trace the history of Masonry from the earliest period of the world's history, the least reflection will convince one that all this has nothing to do with speculative Masonry. Almost all the book having reference to Freemasonry may be said to be in that one paragraph, which is here given:

*A Mason is obliged by his Tenure to obey the moral Law;*

*and if he rightly understands the ART, he will never be a stupid ATHEIST, nor an irreligious LIBERTINE. And though in ancient Times Masons were charged in every Country to be of the Religion of that Country or Nation, whatever it was, yet 'tis now thought more expedient only to obligate them to that Religion in which all Men agree; leaving their particular opinions to themselves; that is, to be GOOD MEN AND TRUE, or Men of Honor and Honesty, by whatever Denomination or Persuasion they may [be] distinguished; whereby Masonry becomes the Center of Unity, and the means of conciliating true Friendship among Persons that must else have remained at a perpetual distance.*

This paragraph may be summed up in a single phrase, which fully expresses the vital spirit of Freemasonry - The Majesty of the Moral Low.

Professor Henry Van Dyke has made the splendid generalization that the aim and purpose of the Shakespearean dramas also is to teach the Majesty of the Moral Law. It will be found, when the plays are studied from this viewpoint, that they form a comprehensive and consistent body of ethics or moral philosophy, the term being used in the Baconian sense as embracing politics, ethics, as commonly conceived, and logic; and that this system is entirely in harmony with the teachings of Freemasonry. It may be more exact to say that Freemasonry is a training school to make the realization of this philosophy possible. Perhaps the simplest and yet most satisfactory definition of Freemasonry is Dr. Hemming's, that: "Freemasonry is a beautiful system of morals, veiled in allegory and illustrated by symbols." Shakespeare may be also defined as a beautiful system of morals, veiled in allegory and illustrated by fictitious and historical personages.

Further, one play, The Tempest, which stands first in the collected plays, is an epitome, a miniature of the whole. The argument of our main proposition - the identity of Shakespeare and Freemasonry - may be based upon the proper interpretation of this play. One primary idea must be kept in mind: these plays are works of art; works of literary art, which, next to music, is the highest art; and again, in the form of the drama, which is the highest form of literary art. And as Alfred Noyes has so aptly expressed it, "The content and import of a work of art are not to be weighed in the same way as those of a philosophic system or a work of science." It is to be realized more as a personal experience, not so much comprehended by the mind as apprehended by the soul. Let it not be thought strange, therefore, if for many persons The Tempest has little significance. For that matter, to how comparatively few persons is Shakespeare anything more than a name. The reason is to be found in our one-sided, unnatural and, in many respects, false education. Others can place themselves where Shakespeare and Freemasonry meet, if they but free their minds from traditions and prejudices.

Hence, to read these plays as mere stories in dramatic form, filled in with many wise reflections, is to miss their real character. The Tempest may be read simply as such a story, and even as having a moral purpose. Sir Edward Strachey says quite aptly that it is "a mimic, magic tempest which we are to see, a tempest raised by art, to work moral ends with actual men and women," But he fails to show how it is to bring about such a state in the actual affairs of men, say of our day or of any time. The play contains hints suggesting that it is meant to be of universal application. It will yet be clear that this play can be fairly interpreted as an allegorical drama, summing up the whole method of Francis Bacon's philosophy, and especially his moral philosophy, as it is to affect in actual life the individual, and all the relations which men and women sustain toward each other, from the primary relations of the family to the highest, which is that of government. And when so interpreted it will be found that it is also the philosophy of Freemasonry.

In a small frame hanging on one of the beautiful marble columns in the Library of the Masonic Temple at Philadelphia Pa. are a number of Masonic Landmarks, which may be accepted as a fair statement of some fundamental principles of Freemasonry. They are reproduced here:

MASONIC LANDMARKS

*The Moral Law is Masonic Law.*

*Obedience to lawful authority is inculcated by Masonry.*

*Masonic qualifications are mental, moral and physical.*

*Masonic preferment is grounded upon real worth and personal merit only*

*Charity should be the distinguishing characteristic of a Mason.*

*The will of the majority governs for the good of the whole.*

*Secrecy is indispensable in Masonry.*

*The Master is the head of the Lodge.*

*In his absence the Wardens preside according to rank.*

*The Grand Lodge is supreme in its sphere of jurisdiction.*

*The approbation of God is the highest Masonic honor.*

Comparing these Masonic Landmarks with The Tempest it can be seen how they are woven into the word-pictures of the play.

As the Moral Law forms the first Landmark, so the main theme of the play is illustrated by the story of the violation of the moral law by the false Duke and his confederates, and their repentance; with the result that a reconciliation of all the persons is brought about, and they agree to live in harmony and unity.

The second landmark is the recognition of lawful authority. Now, the very first scene of the play teaches the same lesson. In the first twenty-seven lines is embodied the whole theory of authority and obedience, as the basis of true liberty. Notice the cheerful obedience of the sailors to the commands of their proper superiors, and the sudden change to sullen opposition to those who had no lawful right to order them about. In the same way it can be seen how the other general abstract principles of Masonry are illustrated as the play progresses.

But it is desired to call special attention to the distinguishing term of Freemasonry - the word Free. Freedom is the enveloping, penetrating atmosphere of the play as a whole, and of every part of it. It is the necessary life-giving principle for the development of the individual and society as therein portrayed. The idea of freedom is present in almost every action of importance throughout the entire play, and forms the theme of a postscript, in form of an apologue. The simple wish of Caliban, type of primitive man, or of the animal becoming human, is for his freedom; and it forms the last wish of Prospero, type of the highest developed man. But above all, the promise of freedom and the hope of attaining it formed the very life of Ariel, and was the spur to all his activity; and Ariel, it is believed, symbolizes the spirit of man.

To analyze the play in detail would make this paper too long. Let this marvelous drama of The Tempest be interpreted as an allegory expressing in the form of literary art what Bacon meant to express in sculpture by the statue of Orpheus, which he erected in his grounds of Gorhambury. The result will show whether it bears such an interpretation and has any relation to Freemasonry.

Bacon inscribed the statue, Philosophy Personified. He interpreted Orpheus as denoting learning, and the ancient fable as a picture of universal philosophy. The music of Orpheus was of two kinds: one that appeased the infernal powers, he applied to natural philosophy, which seeks to understand and control the physical world; the other, which draws together men and beasts, to moral and civil discipline. In other words, Bacon understood Orpheus to have been to the Greeks a civilizing hero, who had induced their ancestors to renounce cannibalism, and taught them the arts and sciences and how to live together. This, Bacon thought, was the true Orpheus music or harmony.

Now, The Tempest presents to us a picture of similar sordid, selfish and warring social conditions transformed into a society where reparation has been made for all injustice, where no man is to "shift" for himself, but where each shall shift for the others, and where, as a result, peace prevails. "The supreme harmony prevails when all things are in harmony with the moral order." The events, which brought this about culminated in the marriage of Miranda, the admired daughter of Prospero, to the prospective reigning prince. This marriage, with its attendant happiness, is emblematic of the prosperity and peace of a state, which would accept Bacon's philosophy, symbolized here by Miranda. It will be noticed that she is the very embodiment of pity, sympathy for her fellow-men, as Ariel is the embodiment of thought, especially in its highest manifestation, that of the creative imagination. Herein lies the explanation of the figure, which represents Freemasonry as spanning the world with its arms of light and love and benevolence. It is indeed a picture of an ideal civilization, of a state requiring a high degree of education to be even approximately realized. This is the invisible Temple, continually being built.

The teachings of Freemasonry lead in this same direction, and I submit that the Order was instituted to bring to pass just such a condition of society, in which Masons are to be the living stones. It was meant to be a civilizing force, working throughout the whole world. The universal application of its principles and teachings attest to this fact. These principles in their general form are embodied in The Tempest, while in the other plays they are exemplified as they apply to the manifold conditions of human relations. It should be said that these plays are extra-institutional, something like the post-graduate studies of schools and colleges. They have no immediate connection with the secret work of the Lodge.

Freemasonry is frequently conceived as a religion. The language of the Ancient Charges implies that it may be so considered. Every religion has its body of doctrines, its votaries, and an organization through which, by means of rituals and worship, these doctrines are taught to its followers and disseminated among outsiders. In Freemasonry the Lodges and the secret work correspond to the religious organizations and their rituals. But Freemasonry has no body of doctrines. Freemasonry is not a matter of belief. Its members are to think and feel and act. And in lieu of a body of doctrines I name the peerless plays of Shakespeare as embodying and exemplifying the principles, which are to serve as a guide and inspiration of Masons; that is, beyond what is inculcated by the secret work of the Lodges.

If an explanation is asked how modern Freemasonry was connected with Operative Masonry, the answer is that the ancient Institution was taken as the wild stock on which the new was grafted, exactly as each of the plays was based on some older tale or legend. The process is set forth quite plainly in that charming play, The Winter's Tale, where the author says:

> *"we marry*
> *A gentler scion to the wildest stock,*
> *And make conceive a bark of baser kind*
> *By bud of nobler race; this is an art*
> *Which does mend nature, change it, rather, but*
> *The art itself is nature."*

The great secrecy and mystery, which surrounded the early history of the Order was necessary to establish it, but this should no longer hold in our day.

It may be that all this is well known in the higher Masonic circles, but kept hid, like so many other things, from motives of prudence. But if such a course seemed necessary at one time in the history of Freemasonry, it is difficult to see a reason for continuing it. If it is not known, then the conviction is expressed that a careful examination will verify the discovery. And its importance cannot be questioned or exaggerated. Freemasonry makes a private appeal to all that is best, noblest and most unselfish in man; and to stimulate the interest by a certain amount of mystery, secrecy of symbolism is well and good. But this has its limitations. In these days many men have advanced beyond such a stage in their education. To them the actual truth cannot fail to appeal. It will solve not only the perplexing question of the authorship of the plays, but in large measure their real meaning, and furnish a practical way of relating them to men's lives, thus making them what they were meant to be - a vital, educating force. It will explain the tremendous spurt of civilization in England during Bacon's lifetime, and make clear who was the intellectual dynamo that furnished not only the light and power of that wonderful period, but the impulse, which led to our present advanced stage of civilization. It will confirm the opinion that Freemasons were meant to be the special guardians and conservators of the richest and noblest treasure intended for the welfare of mankind that the human mind ever collected. It will establish the fact that in modern times lived a philosopher, Francis Bacon, the freest, wisest, most tender of men, who for three centuries has met the common fate of philosophers - to be misunderstood and maligned - but who planned a scheme of philosophy surpassing all that ever preceded; and who also made provision for its dissemination and preservation among men.

Let Freemasonry acknowledge its paternity, which will be found to have been noble in name and most noble in fact, and claim its inheritance, with its attending responsibilities, and it will have the means to solve the difficulties and dispel the fears felt by many members and expressed so forcibly by the good brother, Bishop Charles T. Williams, of Michigan, when he said: "*I have often felt that Freemasonry should be something more than a mere theatrical exhibition, with some technical charity and a good deal of social intercourse; but I do not see just how its moral forces can be effectually concentrated and directed.*" It can also meet the criticism, and fulfill the prophecy presented by Oswald Wirth, who declared that our institution has not yet found itself, that it seeks itself like the youth who is forced to recognize himself, and take knowledge of what he really is. He predicts that an epoch will come forcibly, when all that is respectable will be universally respected - when forms shall be appreciated and scrupulously observed no more by instinct or superstition, but in reason, for what they contain as living.

Let Freemasonry but find itself - and this is possible by the author's last will and testament, The Tempest - and there is nothing that can prevent it from becoming the world-wide civilizing force which it was designed to be, becoming the most potent factor in dispelling ignorance and superstition, in bringing about a fuller freedom and development of man, and in replacing the selfishness, deceit and inhumanity, which unchecked must eventually destroy our civilization, by the rule of justice and love, which alone can unite mankind into a universal brotherhood.

# The Hiramic Legend

"Here lies your Brother no better than the Earth he Lies upon, If he is That which now He is like.....He is Dead."
-*The Tempest*

---

Every Masonic historian has pondered the Story of Hiram and the problem of its incorporation into the crude rite of an operative craft. Beginning with the fatal *assumption that Speculative Freemasonry began in operative Lodges and that the Ethical Cult "evolved"--(ignoring the patent historic fact that the operative gild union was swept away by successive Acts of Parliament before we had a modern language in which a modern Ritual could be imaginatively expressed)* --every Masonic scholar has signally failed to indicate WHO created the Hiram Legend or WHEN it was created.

It is abundantly clear that someone with a knowledge of Hermetic Rites and the Ancient Mysteries created the Story as a piece of imaginative fiction and that it was created in order that it may take the place of the Third Degree Death Rite of the Mysteries......which centered round the Death and Resurrection of their Gods. In those Ancient Days the Candidate took the place of the God as the Initiate does to-day in the Modern Mystery. There is thus a parallel between the Ancient Rite and the Modern One.

Bro. Pike says that in 1717:

"In one of the Four Old Lodges were Squires, Noblemen, Military Officers, Scholars, Philosophers, Clergymen,. To these men must be ascribed the authorship of the Third Degree and the introduction of Hermetic and other Symbols in Masonry."

That scholars were members of such a Lodge is capable of direct proof, but it is not capable of proof that these men-- acting apparently as a Committee --created the THIRD DEGREE. It is pure guess work on the part of Bro. Pike. It is moreover, quite impossible for any heterogeneous Committee to produce a piece of Literature like the Ritual, which is essentially an Art Form of Dramatic Construction bearing the imprint of a single MIND that conceived and technically executed. There has never been a Committee yet that has produced a great Work of Art.

The reader will, however, have already noted that not only has it been proved by direct evidence that there was more than ONE DEGREE worked by the Brethren prior to 1717, but that in the Shakespeare Folio there seems to be circumstantial evidence that suggests a knowledge by the Author of the Hiram Story alleged by Modernists to be unknown prior to 1717.

As a matter of fact, the Masonic commentator who believes that Speculative Masonry grew out of an operative trinitarian formula, cannot even suggest WHY Solomon, the Temple, the Pillars B.... and J.....,the Rites of the Mysteries (what little we know of them), the use of the Sacred Volume, the Three Pillars Wisdom, Strength and Beauty, the Apron of the Mysteries (Jason's Golden Fleece), etc. were ever chosen by the alleged "Gentlemen" or "operatives" to play such an important part in the modern Ceremonial. No one has ever suggested WHY it was done or HOW it happened.

No writer has produced the slightest evidence regarding the IDENTITY of the MAN or MEN who created the THIRD DEGREE. Refuge has been consistently taken in vague statements like Bro. Pike:

"To these men must be ascribed........" etc.

Without a shred of textual, historical or antiquarian evidence. We have the equally airy opinion of Bro. Blackham:

"The whole of the Ritual of the Craft.......developed during the eighteenth century."

Bro. Hobbs is equally emphatic and equally vague:

"During this period--1717 to1735--the Hiramic Legend was Evolved...... 1746 being the probable date when the Royal Arch Ceremony was *arranged."*

Needless to say we are not told WHO "arranged" it, nor is there any evidence forthcoming to pin down the *"Arrangement"* to this particular year. Because we only hear of the Royal Arch Chapter about this period it by no means follows that the Chapter had not been long practiced in secret prior to this date. Its EMERGENCE about 1746 is a proof of the care with which our Ancient Brethren guarded their secrets from "attacks of the insidious." It is absurd really to talk of the Royal Arch being "arranged" in 1746 when there "are clear hints of the Royal Arch *as early as* 1723, the first express reference occurring in 1744."

We have, virtually, little or no knowledge of the "historic" Hiram Abiff who suffered martyrdom by being slain by "THREE MEN OF SIN" at the entrance to the Temple of Solomon. There was a Hiram in the Scriptures who was a Widow's son of the tribe of Naphtali and that is about all we know. He is unknown to Jewish literature and the story of his martrydom is peculiar to Masonry alone. There is no ancient legend respecting him. It has been suggested that the Crusaders brought back the story from the Holy Land, but there is no proof that it was ever in existence save a Masonic Fable. Dr. Oliver says:

"The Third Degree is traditional, historical, legendary.....its tradition being hyperbolical, its history apocryphal, its legends fabulous."

In other words someone specially created a Hiramic Myth--marked with all the detail creative touches of genius; and wove this Myth into the Art of Temple Building, no longer an operative art but a Spiritual Cult based on the sentence: *"Know ye not that ye are the Temples of the Living God."*

Who are the men that create Myths? Who produce our songs? Who wrote the Sagas? Who fabricate "Feigned Stories?" The songs of Badur and Beowulf? The Arthurian Legend ? *The Regius Poem?* Only one type of mind.... the man of imagination. In the old days they were called Minstrels and Poets! Someone with the mind of a Poet--one who was saturated with the Myths of the Ancient World--conceived the idea of creating a modern Rite based on the ancient one. Since he could not introduce a Pagan Christos, he introduced the Holy Temple of the Jew, three Grand Masters, one being the wisest man on earth......."Profound Solomon," a legendary Hiram Abiff and a "Tragedy." That is why the Hiram history is apocryphal! Why we have teachings which bear affinities with the folklore of primitive man! Why there are analogies between our Rites and the Ceremonies of Amen Ra and the Mysteries of Holy Byblos.

"There are ceremonies even more remarkable in character connected with the Royal Arch and certain additional Degrees with other religious observances of antiquity."

One could therefore almost imagine William Shakespeare writing such words as these:

> "For if I should profess that I, going the same road as THE ANCIENTS, have something better to produce, there must needs have been some Comparison or Rivalry between us.... in respect of excellency or ability of wit."

This actually was written by an Elizabethan [Francis Bacon]; and it is a matter for conjecture whether such a sentence as this does not refer to a return along the Road to Antiquity, the Ancient Mysteries which are to be the Model or Type of the New Ethical System of Elizabethan Freemasonry...... a system which will be better than the old one because it will be linked to the Christian idea of Love or Charity.

In any case the Masonic system was created by a man who was an Egyptian in soul, a Greek in heart, a Christ-man by conviction and an Elizabethan in expression. He was one who knew exactly what POESY stood for according to the Elizabethan standard.

This is what Shakespeare says regarding the creating of a poetic fiction around a piece of living history. In *As You Like It*, Act III, s. 5:

Audrey says: "I do not know what Poetical is......*Is it a True Thing?*"

Touchstone: "No!....The Truest Poetry is *the most* FEIGNED. What they may swear in Poetry may be said...... *They do FEIGN.*"

Shakespeare therefore knew that the Poets were the *Inventors* of Historical Tales that were *"feigned."* The writers pretended they were historical (like Shakespeare's Histories), but they were not so *literally,* romance and imagination being mixed liberally with the real facts. He knew this as a truth because he was guilty of this sin..... if "sin" it be.

It must have been a characteristic of the Elizabethan Age because a contemporary, Francis Bacon, wrote similarly:

"By Poesy I mean nothing else than FEIGNED History."

Shakespeare's estimate of true poetry was that in order for it to be lovely,

"There must be matter as well as Art, the spontaneous overflow of a full mind stirred to the brim with true history, a knowledge of nature and especially human nature."

Let it once be conceded that Shakespeare beside being a supreme Artist was also, deliberately, an Ethical Teacher, possessed with a great URGE--"a Philanthropia"--for the Good of Mankind and the door is once open for his active connection with the Elizabethan Fraternity. As a creative artist, of profound knowledge, saturated as every student knows with the wisdom of the East, the theogonies of vanished civilizations, he could have created the Third Degree Death Rite and the Hiram Myth without the slightest difficulty. The Creator of Prospero, Hamlet and Lear could certainly have called Hiram into being and woven around him the tragical setting. I know of no one else in the whole range of literature who could have done so.

In any case, Shakespeare knew the Hiram story--whether he coined it or not--for he leaves it in scattered fragments in various parts of the plays.

www.ingramcontent.com/pod-product-compliance
Lightning Source LLC
LaVergne TN
LVHW041501070426
835507LV00009B/736